THE MICHIGAN DOGMAN
TRUE STORIES FROM EYE WITNESSES

GP HAGGART

Copyright © 2019 by Greg P. Haggart

All rights reserved. No part of this book may be reproduced in any form or by any electronic or mechanical means, including information storage and retrieval systems, without permission in writing from the author, except by a reviewer who may quote brief passages in a review.

First Edition

The names of the witnesses and people in this book have been altered to protect their identities.

ISBN: 9781071398357

Note

This book is not intended to be presented as fact but rather provide the reader to come to their own conclusions. The purpose for this book is to provide an entertaining read of true eyewitness encounters of dogmen in Michigan and to act as an historical record of those encounters. If you have a dogman encounter from Michigan you would like to tell and share with the public feel free to email it to gphaggart1775@gmail.com. We will review your encounter and should we deem it to be plausible we will add it to our book. Thank you.

Introduction

Most of us Michiganians or Michiganders (whichever you prefer) wake up each morning, have our breakfast, drink our coffee, and follow the routine of the drive to work in the morning with our eyes fixed on the road. We work hard for eight to maybe twelve hours and then punch out for the return drive home. We get out of our cars walk into our homes and are greeted by our loving spouses and children. This is our reality as we see it every day, week by week, month by month, and year by year. Did you ever pause for a few seconds, take your eyes off the road to see the forests you travel through? Do you pay attention to the shadows in the parking lot when you leave work late? I bet you do not. To a select few Michianians who were dragged out of their realities and into a world of folklore and legend, coming out of there face to face with experiences of a new sense of how the world works. These eyewitnesses are few but are growing not just in Michigan but around the world. What is it they experience that has left a scar upon their lives that is forever sunken into their skins? It is the dogmen. Yes, that's right, dogmen.

Throughout the world sightings of these creatures are growing in number. Those brave enough to step forward to tell their stories do so to warn others while others do not say a word for fear of slander and the ruin of their good names. They are mocked and doubted but will swear upon a stack of Bibles or on their grandmother's grave they saw what they saw. Witnesses of the dogman come in all shapes and sizes from; the wealthy, teachers, farmers, politicians, scientists, clergy, lumberman, truck drivers, and people like yourself. Many people who are skeptical of the dogman eyewitness accounts won't believe them until they see one…until they see one of course. Myself, I am one of those folks who will believe it when they see it yet can't help but to weigh the evidence that there is something stalking the forests of Michigan. When you really think about it, everyday people do not normally enter the forests. Most of the time people "drive" through forests in Michigan but do they ever stop by the side of the road, get out, and walk through the woods? No. People spend most of their time in cities, small towns, streets, roads, jobs, and in their homes. Never do people spend most of their time in the woods unless their field of practice demands it. What about country folk, you ask? As a country boy through and through I can tell you that most country folk spend most of their time in the house, garage, or the yard and rarely walk through the woods unless you are a child; which of course a lot of children will claim to see odd things in the woods even claiming to see dogmen. On average the one time of the year when most Michiganians are in the woods are during the months of October and December and even then some hunters come out seeing a dogman. It is possible there are more sightings of dogmen in Michigan during hunting season than there is any other time of the year. Yet with all the skeptics many people do not wish to come forward and tell their stories for fear of being criticized.

    In addition, I myself am a skeptic but I find the many reports and eye witness accounts of this bipedal beast to be fascinating. Is it real? Does it exist or is there some sort of major hoax doing on? Are eye witnesses actually mistaking these creatures for some other animal? With so many people not just in Michigan but in other states and around the world sending in reports of seeing dogmen it can be kind of hard to ignore the reports. The internet makes it easy for people to communicate and to post their photos and stories; including those reports proven to be frauds. The first report by white English settlers in Michigan of a dogman was in 1887 in Wexford County. According to the legend two lumberjacks saw the creature and described it as a seven-foot tall, blue-eyed, or amber-eyed bipedal canine-like animal with the torso of a man and a fearsome howl that sounded like a human scream. In 1937 in Paris, Michigan, Robert Fortney was attacked by five wild dogs and said one of the five walked on two legs. Reports of similar creatures also came from Allegan County in the 1950s, and in Manistee and Cross Village in 1967. In 1987 disc jockey Steve Cook at WTCM-FM in Traverse City, Michigan recorded a song titled "The Legend", which he initially played as an April Fool's Day joke. He based the song on myths and legends from around North America, and had never heard of an actual Michigan "dogman" at the time of the recording stating, "I made it up completely from my own imagination as an April Fools' prank for the radio and stumbled my way to a legend that goes back all the way to Native American times." In an area in Arenac County called the Omer Plains, native Americans believe there are wolf-like spirit beings we call today as, "The Witchie Wolves," who come out at night and protect the land. Teenagers around the Saginaw Bay area will travel up to the Omer Plains area and run from car to car to try and out run these wolf spirits. Some teenagers say they were not so lucky and could feel something grab or bite onto their legs while they ran. Others claim they will hear barking behind them while running from car to car.

In like manner, reports of dogman-like creatures are not just found in Michigan. Reports come in from all over the world of people seeing dogmen, even in other states. One popular report among dogman investigators comes out of Kentucky in a region known as the LBL (Land Between the Lakes) in the early 80's could not be ignored and still to this day is talked about among the cryptozoology community. The report states: one evening a family of four drove into a camping ground in the LBL. The father was leveling the RV while his son was nearby when he got on all fours by his RV and then looked up to see a creature towering over him. The creature, a dogman, had ripped his head off, the young boy ran for his life toward the RV door. To see what the commotion was all about the mother came to the door and to her horror watched the dogman kill her son while he tried to flew to the safety of the RV. Police stated they believed the woman's motherly instincts took over to defend her daughter who had locked herself in the closet. The police claim the mother put up a good fight against the creature since her nails were torn off down to the bone when her body was found. Police said the inside of the RV looked like a meat locker, and they believed the dogman had found the little girl, ripped off the door and took her. Believing the girl may still be alive a man hunt for her began and they later found her body hanging in a tree. Local Army special forces were called in after police realized what they were dealing with was an apex predator of some kind. The army finally found and killed the animal which killed the family and the whole thing came under wraps. When you try to find out more information about the case it is as if the whole thing never happened yet there have been authorities from the area who have came forward stating the event actually occurred. Many posed the question asking why the authorities were covering up the incident when dogman investigators came to the conclusion if the public knew these creatures were out there then no one would enter public parks and would affect economic growth in those areas. Yet others believe the federal and state government know about these creatures and deliberately cover up their existence for fear of public outcry and dangerous manhunts of the creatures would occur causing the deaths of hundreds. In several missing persons cases involving children along the pacific states FBI agents have been called in but the mysterious thing about these cases is the fact that the FBI does not handle missing persons cases. So the question remains; why was a federal government agency involved who had no business these cases? In these missing persons cases when the child is found alive fifty to hundred miles away and later questioned, the survivors can only recall being carried away in the woods or hypnotised to enter the woods only later to awaken in another location alone. How were these children from ages 4 to 6 able to trek miles through the woods only to show up days later at another location? The other mystery that causes investigators to question government knowledge of these creatures are their reports when a person dies from an animal attack. There have been cases where such reports will state, "unknown animal," yet each state has their own department of natural resources that can clearly identity the type of animal that attacked the deceased. They know a bear will maul, and a wolf will go for the throat, so why is it "unknown?" quite possibly the answer could be because they have never seen such an animal do such horrific damage to a human body.

    Moreover, eye witnesses of the creatures have stated how the environment changes when a dogman is near. First, all sound in the forest disappears; you can hear a pin drop. Next there is an intense feeling of being watched. Once the creature is spotted witnesses state it stares at you and you can't comprehend what it is. Others say your first reaction is shock and your brain cannot process the creature once it stands up on two legs, then the primal fear hits as you realize you are no longer at the top of the food chain. In addition, there is a strange popping or snapping sound of bones when the creature begins standing up on its hind two legs. Witnesses claim the beast is as ripped as a bodybuilder in the chest and shoulders with man-like hands and dog or wolf-like legs. The head is enormous and impossible to understand how the legs can support all that weight. In all of the eye witness accounts I have studied every person who sees the beast in its entirety is in utter awe over how massive, evil, and breathtaking it is. But is it real? How is a creature that appears to be half-man, half-wolf in appearance able to exist, if it does? Some investigators believe it is dinopithecus, meaning "terrible ape" a giant baboon, other investigators say the creature is new and does not show up in the fossil record, while there are those who say they are actual werewolves; people who have become cursed with demons and walk the earth feeding on flesh.

    What do you think? Enclosed in this book are the short accounts from a few people in Michigan who have either encountered or saw the beasts with their naked eye. These are not every encounter that happened in Michigan but rather only a few who have come forward to tell their tales. Each of the accounts have had their names removed to protect their identities. Following the accounts are witness photos and images taken from videos from around the world of dog-like creatures by unsuspecting victims who ran into the creatures and lived to tell their tales. I am not saying the beasts are real but I am only saying, there is something strange about this. I only ask that you do your own research into the Michigan Dogman, search the web and come to your own conclusion.

    Join me on this quest to investigate the Michigan Dogman, our state's most terrifying cryptid. To see if the legend is true, and to find out for sure if there is something out there, in the woods, hunting through the night, watching us from Michigan's forests, and traversing the state's residential areas from the shadows.

Variances of Dogmen

Most people who have never seen a dogman will usually imagine the creature as a wolf or dog size beast with the ability to walk on its hind legs. This is not always the case as you will learn the variances of dogmen. According to most cryptozoologists, there are seven variants. When all documented dogman sightings are compiled we can see they come in all shapes in sizes but one thing is generally the same; the snout.

Type 3's
Type 3 dogmen can range in color from black, grey, brown, and even orange. One thing to remember is type three dogmen have legs and knees like a human. Type three's are generally more ape-like in appearance yet have a snout. They have been mistaken at times for a sasquatch but what separates them from the sasquatch are snouts.

Type 3 Variant 1 - is tall, lean, strong and has a baboon style head. This kind of dogman is what allows some researchers to believe dogmen are dinopithecus; a giant baboon.

Type 3 Variant 2 - Hominid body, chow-like head. Because of their human-like appearance they are often mistaken for werewolves.

Type 3 Variant 3 - Sasquatch with a muzzle. Hair can be puffy in appearance and are often mistaken for a bigfoot.

Canine Types
The canine type dogman resembles more of the werewolf in present day horror movies like Underworld and Van Helsing. Not only do they have human-like features but have canine as well. Their heads are said to be huge looking like a canine, chest built like a bodybuilder with a more thinner appearance, human-like hands with two to three inch claws, and the hind legs of a canine. The normal height ranges are between seven to ten feet tall.

Canine Variant-1 - Like a standing timber wolf, and the thinnest of all the canine variants. Witnesses have said it looks exactly like a timber wolf but is able to stand up on its hind legs. Hair color is often black, brown, white, or grey.

Canine Variant-2 - Hyena-like and is best known for it's rough and menacing-like features, having been seen with spots on them like a hyena. It is unknown if this type of dogman keeps it's calls like a hyena. Colors range from black and brown. Often spotted with the appearance like it is smiling.

Canine Variant 3 - Large, strong bodied, pointy ears, and are the most commonly seen dogmen. This type is much taller, built like a bodybuilder, athletic structure, muscular, and resemble the werewolves in the movies Underworld, Van Helsing, and even Dog Soldiers.

Canine Variant-4 - Soldier, extremely large head, or what some eye witnesses have said to be a fat head which is unusually unfitting for the body. They are known to be more aggressive, have been known to kill other dogmen, and are believed to be a more superior type. They are much taller, leaner, and muscular than other dogmen. The color of these dogmen range from black to grey.

Lights and Dogmen

In some cases lights are associated with some sightings of dogmen; not necessarily UFO's but odd bright orb-like lights. One such notable case was an episode of Paranormal Witness on the SyFy channel titled, The Wolf Pack. Before the family's encounter with five dogmen in the state of Maine they saw strange lights in the woods from their house. In some cases of dogmen, strange lights are viewed either before or after the sighting. As you will read from the following dogman encounters witnesses may describe seeing strange lights.

DOGMAN SIGHTINGS

Dogman Sighting, 1994

This encounter took place in the area of Watersmeet, home of the famous Paulding Lights phenomenon. Oddly enough, the Paulding Lights are also known as the "Dog Meadow Lights":

"I was thirteen, had just gotten new roller-blades for Christmas and, since the main road where our property sits is paved, I couldn't wait to ride around. I went blading by myself and stopped to rest for a second. On this road, the woods are so thick, there's not much space between the road and the woods in most parts, and I remember seeing trees pushed down on the road that my dad said was done by bears. (He was an avid bear hunter) I remember not hearing any of your normal sounds of nature, not even birds. The air was still, and the sky would be pure dark in not too long. I was deciding to turn back, when I heard a rustling behind me, and something emerge from the left side of the road. I assumed it was a deer, and paused and made myself as quiet as I could so I could watch it, and slumped down on my stomach in the middle of the road. It was about six hundred feet ahead of me.

"When I got myself settled in the road to watch it and looked up, I realized what I was looking at wasn't a deer. It was on all fours, with grey/brown fur. At first, I feared the worst, thinking a bear had caught my scent, until I saw it's outline and color. I thought I was looking at a dog until I realized the face was too... primitive? Like a fox or a coyote's. At this point in my life, I had never seen a wolf in real life, and it was too far for me to make out the face exactly."

"... it extended it's front legs, and in the slowest, longest seconds of my life, stood up on it's hind legs, sniffed the air, walked for about five steps. Then got back down on all fours and walked to the other side of the woods, then disappeared.

"I don't remember how long I laid in the middle of the road staring in the empty space I saw this thing stand like a human. I remember my jaw hanging down as low as it could, and a pool of drool on the cement under it. It finally clicked in my mind that, perhaps, I should roller-blade my butt back to camp as quick as I could."

Dogman crossed road, Tioga River, 2008

Last fall, my son and I were driving on US-41/M-28 towards Three Lakes in Michigan's Upper Peninsula (where I live). The beast ran across the highway near Tioga Creek. I had not heard of this before reading Phantoms and Monsters, but this is exactly what we saw. We are familiar with all animals living here. Moose regularly cross in front of drivers, so we watch the sides of the roads carefully. We were very puzzled and thought it might be some mutant wolf and could not figure out what we witnessed. It ran fairly fast about 50 feet in front of our truck. It was so strange because the front of it was much higher up than the back, larger than a wolf

"Type 3" Dogman sighting, 2011

I was driving north on Craig Lake Rd. towards Teddy Lake. As I approached Nestoria Rd. I noticed something move off the edge of the road into the woods. It was around 6:30 am and a little bit dewy and foggy at that time but I definitely saw something move. I stopped at the intersection and watched across Nestoria Rd. I first thought it was a moose but this was too agile.

I took a slow left turn and looked to my right into the woods. I didn't see anything so I looked forward and sped up. Immediately, this animal ran out of the woods in front of my car and jumped across the road to the south side. I mean it took 3 long strides and was gone - almost like it vanished through an invisible wall!

I was shocked. I continued driving for a few minutes but had to pull off and stop. I was literally shaking from head to toe. I sat there wondering what that was. It was on all fours and had back legs like those of a large man. It had jet black fur and looked like a very large wolf other than the back legs and the human-like rump. There was no tail. The profile of the head and snout were that of a wolf. It didn't make a sound.

Huge quadruped with orange eyes and UFO

On I-75, a couple hundred yards south of the Bay Road overpass in Mackinac County, I noticed something move near the highway reflectors. Thinking it was a deer I turned on the bright lights and watched for it to cross the road. As I approached it I notice that what I thought was the reflectors on the highway was orange, and then it blinked on and off like an eye. Thinking, "what the heck is that?" I sped up to get closer. As I got closer I could see the silhouette of the animal. It was sitting like a dog, its head was even with the reflectors. It stood on all 4s and turned and walked down in the ditch then up a little incline then turned and looked at my truck. It turned back to the highway walked on all 4s to the shoulder of the blacktop looked at the truck again with those orange eyes. The eyes were huge. It then jumped to within a foot or two of the center line, and then the next jump landed in the grass on the shoulder of the road. I was probably like 100 feet from it. This animal was rippling in muscles, and looked like it weighed around 500 pounds if not more. Its hair which covered its body looked short and its head was huge with hardly no neck. After I passed where it crossed I hit the brakes, as there were no cars on the highway, and started to back up. As I got close to the spot where it crossed I suddenly felt fear and thought, "What the hell am I doing?" I put the truck back in drive and began to leave. As I was rolling the window up I glanced back and noticed a light, bright like a flood light, ascending into the sky at a high rate of speed. It was at a angle of about 1 o'clock and in just a few seconds was out of sight. Something else that was strange was there were not any light rays trailing it.

Several dogmen stalking men, 2010

We got maybe 300 yards back in it and started hearing heavy breathing and snapping sounds in the thick brush to our right. We thought maybe coyotes but we got to a corner and were stopped in our track. In front of us, maybe 60 yards away, was something blacker than the woods standing on two feet and stood between 6'8" and 7'4". We slowly turned away and back tracked. Before we got to the field the same thing was in front of us again. We turned around for a second and then turned back...it was gone.

When we got into the field we noticed there were four or more of these creatures, one on each corner of the field just standing there. We saw one move halfway behind a tree. At this point we were freaking out. We made our way through the field and got to the edge and there was one standing directly in the middle of the trail entering the woods. We hauled butt back home and the whole way we felt like we were being watched and stalked.

We have been out every night since then. We have learned do not use lights because it comes closer than 60 yards. The closest it has been to me was maybe 25 yards and was moving closer. At that point I shot at it. There were five total that we saw the first night and after I shot at one. We went out last night and there were only four and they seemed more aggressive. In the field, it seems they tried herding us into a corner.

Dogman sighting, canoe, 1975

There are many trails that run through here. In this area is a place called The Sandies, where all the young kids would go and party. My dad and two of his buddies were in a canoe in broad daylight paddling from The Sandies around the back of the cemetery. The banks of the river are ten to twelve feet high in places, and some trails run right to the edge.

"The three of them saw what looked to be a big dog running behind them on the trail. They didn't pay much attention to it until they heard a splash. When they looked it was swimming after them, then it went from a dog paddle to the chest and front legs coming out of the water and wading after them. They decided right then not to wait around to see what it was.

Possible Dogman climbed tree, 1973

Summer 1973, my dad had just graduated from high school (Waterford Twp High) and he and a bunch of friends had gone up north a ways outside of Traverse City, MI. His friend Susie's (made up name because he doesn't remember) family had a cabin out on a lake up north. There was a group of about 10-12 17-19 year olds all hanging out and drinking beers and celebrating the summer.

The group of them were having a bonfire out on the beach when Susie got up to go to bathroom. My dad's friend, Mike (not made up, family friend who confirms the story) offers to "walk her there" and as they are walking the 50ft from the beach bonfire to the cabin, Susie notices a dark shadow much further up the road near the treeline. Susie points it out to Mike and Mike looks and says they should hurry up because he thinks it might be a bear.

But Mike pauses for a moment as this creature continues to lope closer toward the cabin (but not in a way that indicated it's destination was the cabin), he notices it isn't nearly big enough to be a bear and thinks it may be a wolf of some kind. Susie comments that it doesn't look furry enough and maybe it has mange or is rabid.

As they are walking closer to the cabin, the creature meets a break in the treeline and becomes considerably more visible in the moonlight. That's when Mike calls my dad and another guy over and they see what appears to be a (very) hairy naked man loping down the gravel road on all fours at a pretty decent clip. They send Susie back to the bonfire to be with the rest of the group and they decide to "chase the fucker". (drunk teenaged boys, who knew?)

They start booking it toward this creature. When it sees them heading for it, the creature starts booking it back up the road and across the clearing. Now, my dad ran track and was at the best shape of his damn life, albeit drunk and he couldn't catch the damn thing as it barrelled down a gravel road on all fours. It reaches the tree line and leaps up a clear 10-15ft into a tree.

At this point, a bunch of the beach kids have run over to where the boys all were and there they all saw this weird ape man (as my dad always described him) sitting in the middle of a Spruce tree that it somehow managed to jump up into and climb while butt ass naked.

They toss some beer cans and rocks at the thing and kind of just aggravate it for a few minutes in the darkness when suddenly it emits this horrifying sound. My dad says it was the most blood curdling noise he'd ever heard and it sounds halfway between the bark of a dog and the bleet of a sheep and it was LOUD. After it makes this noise, it starts shaking and sorta of jumping in the tree and then jumps out and books it into the woods.

My dad still swears to me the story is true and Mike has confirmed at least pieces of the story he can remember. As adults me and my dad have discussed our theories and I have just assumed it was a burnt out hippie that had taken too much acid and my dad says that wasn't that rare in that area of Michigan in 73. I'd also like to stress that me and my dad have never heard about the dogman (he really liked that song, btw!) and we had always called him the "ape man".

Dogman sighting near Bendon, 2007

As he approached further, he stated that the only way he could describe the creature was being similar to a very large dark wolf, however he observed that this thing wasn't on four legs, but was upright his back two legs standing near a road killed deer. He estimated that the creature stood a little over six feet tall and had very dark fur.

Dogman charged at car

It was about eight years ago when a couple friends and me were out shining a field off of Summit City road in Kingsley, Michigan. We shined towards the field coming down the road and turned around to shine it again we hit the middle of the field and something stood up and started to run towards us very fast across the field! I hit the gas and there was about 200 yards of field between us and it. It stood up and started to run toward us and when I hit the end of the field, it was 20 – 30 feet away from the side of the truck. I looked down and I was at 60 mph. Very scary. I never look back and never went back and that goes for all of us in the truck.

Near Roscommon, Upright 7' Dogman

We put our stuff in the back of the truck. My buddy heard some rustling in the woods behind us. So me and my buddy got our flashlights out of the truck and when we shined our light into the brush, we saw two huge red glowing eyes about 7 feet up off the ground. We followed them down and all we could see was a massive dog's foot sticking out of the brush so we ran to the truck in fear. When the lights turned on we saw a dog that stood upright about 7 feet tall and we started driving away and we never saw it again and it had to be the scariest experience of our lives.

Huge Dogman spooks camper, 1999

When I was hiking the Au Sable in the summer of 1999. in the counties Oscoda, Alcona and Iosco. I remember one of my most scariest encounters with the wilderness.

while walking east down along the river around 1 hr. prior to dusk I heard what to my ears to be a wolf howl.. I Have seen wolf prints and seen wolves at my home Long Lake MI. but never have I heard a howl so deep and almost human-like in my life.. I got spooked and set up camp and made a fire. larger than most. due to my fear.. At dusk I heard it closer. directly across the river. I had heard stories of the wolfman from native powwows and in family folklore covering the whole USA. But never have I personally seen what I saw that night or the next day. that night after eating beef barley stew from my canned good collection. I laid down by the fire with my huge folding knife closely gripped by my chest. I was watching and listening to the surrounding wood line for about 30 minutes. when the average noises stopped. which to me meant 2 things 1: something had spooked the local animals. and 2: made me very uneasy. I looked out away from the fire and shot the fire away from my eyes using the unarmed hand. I looked across the river which was only about 100 meters across from my fire. and saw the most unnerving sight ever. on the sand was a creature standing may be larger than the average sow black bear, with black fur, large long skull and yellow reflecting eyes like the wolf.. I closed my eyes and hoped I was imagining things and then it gave out the howl again. I opened my eyes and it ran up the bank and disappeared into the night. as it ran it didn't run on all fours like a bear nor a wolf. and unlike the local bigfoot it wasn't full upright like a human or primate.. I was so scared that I slept the rest of that night in a damn tree about 20 foot off the ground. it took me 3 hrs and praying to ease my fear so I could sleep...

Wexford Co. loggers sighting, 1887

Two lumberjacks saw a creature whom they described as having a man's body and a dog's head. This was the first reported dogman sighting in Michigan which has sparked national sightings of the creatures in other states. Not only was this report the first for the state of Michigan but it was the first in the United States.

Manistee Co, Horrendous howl, 1975

I never saw it, but in 1975, I was newly married, about 21 years old, and had a small baby. My sister, who was a teenager, was visiting us. My husband, my sister, and I had all gone to our bedrooms, to settle down and go to sleep. I would say it was around 11 or 12, at night.

We were just starting to relax and get sleepy, when out of nowhere, there was this HORRIBLE, LOUD howl/yell. I mean, it was so loud, it made my chest vibrate and my ears hurt. The sound was not human, but had a gutteral human-like sound, mixed with what sounded like a wolf. We were living in a mobile home at the time and it howled just outside our back door, in the hallway, near our bedroom.

We jumped out of bed, looked at each other, and both said at the same time, "What the hell was that?" My husband was 10 years older than I was and was an avid hunter. He wasn't the kind of guy to scare easily. His face drained of color. My sister came running down the hallway, white as a ghost, and said, "What was THAT?" I told her I didn't know. My husband said he was getting his rifle and grabbed it out of the closet. He opened up the back door and yelled out into the wind, "You better get the $%^$ out of here, or I will blow your head off!" He listened a moment before I yelled at him to please shut the door. He did and we never heard anymore after that.

Needless to say, we stayed up all night, afraid to go to sleep.

Swimming dogman tried to climb into boat, 1967

Gillispie told Wissner that he heard one story from an old lumberman who had gotten it from two friends of his. Gillispie was able to record the gist of their story.

They had been fishing near Manistee on Claybank Lake one day just as the sun was setting, when an animal swimming toward their boat caught their attention. Taking it to be a coon hound that one of them owned, they ignored it until it got close. It was at that point the two men realized that the "swimmer" had a dog's head and a man's body! The men, very frightened, did the natural thing and began to row away.

Dogman rummaging truck's bed

The morning of my encounter I had gotten up a little earlier than usual and was very groggy. I stumbled to the large plate glass window and saw something rummaging in the truck's bed over the side of the truck. I assumed it was just dad so I banged on the window to get his attention and wave. I was chilled to the bone by what peered back at me. A creature that stood on two feet but for the life of me had the head of a dog; canine-like but yet somehow human. We locked eyes for what seemed to be an eternity. Strangely enough though the eyes were not yellow as everyone else seems to see. They were a pale yellow/green in color.

Dogman near Luther

Our family of five lived in a small two room cabin in Michigan. One night my parents had gone out and had an older cousin of mine stay with my younger brother, sister and me. We always had dogs growing up – mainly St. Bernard's & large dogs. It was pretty late at night, my siblings were asleep and my cousin and I were eating ice cream and watching a movie. All of the dogs were out on their chains. First, we heard the neighbor dogs going nuts, barking and growling for a few minutes. Then our four dogs were doing the same. The sounds were hair raising! In the window across the room, both of us seen a very, very tall, hair covered creature peering in at us. It was standing on two legs and looked unnaturally giant- like. It made very low but audible strange noises. We were both so scared that we could not move. Tears poured from my widely open eyes. I have never been so scared or uncomfortable in my whole life!!

Dogman near Luther 2

My friend and I decided to take a bike ride one night, up near Luther. We had just reached a little bit down our road and she suggested turning onto one of the twisting dirt roads next to us. I agreed, and we started down it. Our flashlights were already dim, and when hers went out, we turned around. I suddenly heard a crack, and shone the flashlight in that direction. I caught sight of a man, for my flashlight only reached the bottom of him. I heard a growl and then it moved, disappearing. We raced home, but my friend refused to believe that we'd seen the Dogman. But I was convinced we had.

Dogman sighting in and outside a barn, 1993

Courtney was a teenager at the time, and was sneaking cigarettes behind her parents' home, near Todd Lake northeast of Reed City. The sun was setting on a clear, cold winter day. Courtney was facing a large abandoned barn on the property next door. Through a hole broken in the siding, she saw what she thought was "a piece of old farm machinery," just inside the building.

She watched for a few moments, but the object didn't move. Then a deer or some other large animal snapped a branch in the woods nearby. Courtney's attention was diverted, and she turned her head to see what had caused the noise. In her peripheral vision, she noted that "the farm machinery moved too." When she looked back, the setting sun was silhouetting the object in the barn. She froze in place when she realized that she was looking at a tall animal. It turned its head back and looked straight at her. It was, in Courtney's words, "at least 6 feet tall if not more. It was dark colored. It had a dog like appearance; pointy nose and really big pointy ears."

Courtney dashed into her house to grab a flashlight. When she returned outside, she shined it toward the barn door but the animal was no longer there. She walked closer to the barn to look for tracks in the heavy snow. When she didn't see any, she realized the creature might still be inside, and ran back to the safety of the house. She never saw the creature again.

Courtney later talked to a friend who had seen something "the size of a buffalo but the shape of a dog" in the same barn, but at a different time. The girl had been hysterical for days after her encounter. Neither of these witnesses heard of "The Legend" song, or about the Michigan Dogman, until years later.

Sighting of big reddish-brown dogman, August '94

In August 1994 I saw a dogman cross US 10 near tubelite, a factory i worked at. It was 0445 am and I was heading west on US 10 going to the gas station to get coffee in the morning and it ran from right to left across the road, stopped on the other side and turned around and showed its teeth to me, then, moving swiftly and awesomely, it took off at a amazing speed and it was on 2 legs nearly the whole time. It was about 7 feet tall 350 to 400 lbs., brownish-reddish with some other colors in it.. It clearly had ears sticking up.

Dogman with coyotes, 2008

I was hunting in the fall on private property near Tiff Lake. I usually went to my blind at night like 2 am and slept there till morning. This was late October 2008. It woke me up while I was sleeping in the shanty, and was with 3 coyotes or young dogmen. It actually spoke and gave me a message, telepathically. I fired a shot to scare away the creature but not at it and it vanished. It didn't run away, it vanished.. The coyotes did run though. I never intended to harm it and it knew that.

Eberhart Ave, Red-eyed Dogman with metal-like teeth, 2005

I had just turned onto Eberhart Rd. which is a dirt road from Beaverton Rd. I was traveling south on Eberhart, and going slow as I had just turned the corner, when I spotted the creature on the right hand side of the road, under a yard light that someone had placed at the end of their driveway.
At first I was unable to tell what it was, only that it was large and seemed out of place. In that area of the world we have many deer, and raccoons, rabbits, and the occasional coyote, wolf, mountain lion or bear. But even from a distance and with it hunched over, I could tell this was out of the ordinary.
I slowed my car to a stop as I approached the creature, at this point I still had not seen its face as it was hunched over eating the garbage that had been placed by the side of the road for pick up the following morning. The visibility was good, as the home had installed a yard light, at the junction of the road and their driveway, and the garbage and the creature were directly under it.
The first thing I noticed about the creature was that the fur was very short, like a horse's or a greyhound's, and shiny. The second thing I noticed was that it was in an odd position as it appeared to be hunched down with its arms and face low to the ground, as it was eating garbage, and it had shoulders like a man. It was jet black, and very and I cannot stress this enough, very heavily muscled, as it ate I could see the muscles in its shoulders and arms moving under the skin. It was larger than a man, perhaps the size of a bear when hunched over. If I

had to guess, when fully standing, I would assume it to be over seven feet tall.

At this point my mind was going a million miles an hour trying to identify this creature, the fur and shape was like nothing I had ever seen. Then it looked up, and I still get goose bumps to this day when I remember that face. Its face was horrible, I mean really horrible. The eyes were red, like a sort of red that appeared to give off its own luminescence, this could be incorrect and it could have been that they were just incredibly reflective from the yard light, but he was looking at me, not up, so it was very odd to me that they should glow like that. The teeth were the most predominant feature, they looked so unreal that I stared until it moved trying to convince myself that I was seeing it wrong and there was a logical explanation. The face was shorter than most werewolf or dog man images, and the teeth were so large that it seemed impossible that such a thing could exist. It was hideous, and so terrifying. It had ears like a doberman but they curled in slightly, and it was sitting back on its heals, and it was built like a man from the chest up, shoulders and all. Then it made a lunge of sorts towards the car, the last thing I saw before flooring it out of there, was the face twisting into a snarl and that it was coming towards me.

I have spent years trying to fathom how anything with teeth like that could possibly be a living thing, they just seem like they would get in the way, if that makes any sense. I have also spent years trying to convince myself that his teeth appeared metal due to the reflection of the lights, but Linda, and I could be wrong, but it looked like his teeth shone like metal.

Robert Fortney sighting, 1938

Fear gripped Robert Fortney as he shot and killed one of five dogs that lunged at him as he stood on the banks of the Muskegon River in 1938," wrote Sheila Wissner in the Record-Eagle on April 25, 1987. "But fear escalated to cold terror as the only dog that didn't run off reared up on its hind legs and stared at Fortney with slanted, evil eyes and the hint of a grin." Wissner said the man from Cadillac, Michigan, found himself recalling that traumatic incident when he listened to "The Legend." Fortney's encounter took place near Paris, Mecosta

County, which lies about halfway between Lake Michigan and Saginaw Bay. Although Fortney said he "wouldn't want to call it a dogman," neither did he know WHAT to call the black canid that fearlessly locked eyeballs with him.

Night watchman's photo, 1961

He drew his gun and watched for a few minutes. That's when he noticed this was not a person at all, but something much taller. He said it appeared to be covered in brown/grey hair. It had very broad shoulders and a powerful chest. It alternated between walking on four legs, then standing up on two. He said it seemed to be looking for something along the driveway. He said later he couldn't quite believe what he was seeing. He quietly moved into the house and grabbed his Kodak Signet 35mm camera, which was his pride and joy. At this point I should mention that dad was quite a photography buff. His father had owned one of the first camera stores in Ohio, and dad got the shutterbug from grandpa.

Saginaw Co. Stalking Dogman, 2009

I was arriving home, to my apartment, at 11:45 PM, when I felt a presence by the wood line. I saw something looking at me and then finally, I saw these two eyes. It seemed like it was stalking me. I could only see eyes and the shape of its head. I really couldn't see its body but instantly, I felt fear and went inside my apartment. When I went inside, I started looking through the blinds, just a little bit. I didn't want to move the blinds that much because I knew he knew where I was, so I didn't want to move the window blinds. Then, I saw it heading my way. This beast looked like a bodybuilder, with a wolf or dog-like head. Because of its silhouette, this thing must have been 7 to 8 feet tall.

Cornfield dogman, 2003

In 2003 I was a Schwann guy in Wynn Michigan. The locals told me about a corn monster on West Coe road.They seemed concerned that I was there late at nite.Sometimes at dark it seemed as if something reached out of the weeds towards my truck as I drove by. There was a spot where I would stop to take a break because in a 14 hour day there was certain spots you would count on if you had to take a lunch on the road..this spot was on West Coe Rd.it was a road no one traveled. about 2pm, I stopped my truck pulled it into the brush and ate my lunch. After lunch I stepped out of my truck and stretched.out of the corn five feet in front of me something appeared. It looked unexplainable. Dark, dirty manlike I had been stopping here for 9 months. I yelled jumped in my truck, it just watched me drive past I was scared it jumped on my slow moving truck, this was broad daylight I can still picture it in my mind.

Oceana Co. Several Dogman encounters, 2005

Something was walking out there. The features were canine; legs were shaped like a wolf, bushy tail, everything. But, it was way too tall to be a regular dog or even a wolf, it stood a bit higher than a deer and it was very thin. I only caught the back end of it walking behind a lilac bush, but it was enough for me. I calmly told my friend that we needed to go inside. I told her to walk slowly, since i live in the middle of no man's land, i know that wild animals are attracted to fast moving objects, and the last thing i wanted was to get up close and personal with whatever that thing was."

White dog, size of bear & shaking camper, 2010

In the summer of 2010, I went camping with some of my friends at their cabin near Shelby, Michigan. Some of their cousins came too, so the night after we got there, I was sitting by the fire telling one of them a ghost story. We were right next to a little creek and on the other side of it, a huge, "ghostly" white dog ran by, like it was chasing something. I thought it might be someones runaway pet, but this thing was huge. It was the size of a black bear and it was built like a wolf. So we went across the creek as soon as the wolf thing was gone to look for tracks or anything. We didn't find anything, even in the wet mud.

Later that night, after everybody else went to their own campers (yeah, we were staying in campers even when there's a cabin right there) it was really late, about three in the morning, when the camper started shaking so violently it woke me up. I heard a really low, deep growling right outside the window I was sleeping under. Then the camper started shaking again, and the eerie growling continued. I knew it couldn't be storming out because there wasn't a cloud in the sky before or after that night. When we got back home, we found scratches that looked like claw marks about seven feet off the ground right above the window.

Dogman rushes highway and rams pickup, 2009

One night, she was driving me home. It was very late, well after 11 pm. We were on US-31 Northbound, around the Rothbury area of Oceana County, on the expressway. Being February, in Michigan, the roads were naturally snowy, with scattered patches of ice and bare pavement. There was a small pickup truck in front of us, about 5 car lengths ahead of her car, when all of a sudden, we saw something on 2 legs dart out from the left, just in front of an overpass. It ran across the 2 lane highway and hit the back of the small pickup in the rear quarter-panel, causing the pickup to fishtail. Luckily, the driver of the small pickup regained control but they didn't stop to see what collided with their truck. If anything, it seemed to pick-up speed and get the heck out of there. My friend and I watched in utter astonishment as the creature finished running to the right and disappeared into the weeds and trees along the highway. It didn't even break stride after it hit the truck. We looked at one another, sat in silence for a moment, and then I said, "Did you see….?" She said, "Yea. I saw it…."

We finished the ride to my house in silence; both lost in our thoughts. It looked like a giant dog or wolf. It was on its hind legs; not all 4's and it was at least 7 feet tall. It had pointed ears, a kind of mane around its neck (much like a lion's mane), was dark in color, and its hind legs looked like a dog's, which was even more pronounced, as it was running only on its hind legs. It's front legs were freely swinging as it ran and it seemed to have its mouth slightly open. It had an elongated face, very much like a collie face and a long nose protruding from its face. Its face was covered by longish hair. The entire creature seemed to be covered in long hair but I can't recall if it had a tail.

Dogman digging in creek bank, 2016

I rounded a bend in the crick when up ahead about 55 yards is what looked to be the back of a black bear that was digging into the bank of the crick.

As I was setting my firearm down on one of the little islands in the crick I snapped a branch and it stopped completely what it was doing. I froze and watched as this thing stood up on two legs and started to turn around towards me. It stood 8 feet tall and had a huge wolf like head, snout and ears of a dog, and all black fur. In the first encounter the creature's fur was grey in color with some white, this one was all black.

It kept glancing over to the east and back towards me. It had not yet seen me, it put its snout into the air and looked like it was sniffing the wind. I'm completely freaking out at this point and reach to pick up my firearm to get out of the area quickly when there was a splash up the creek I looked up and now this thing was on all four legs, it still stood 5 to 5 1/2 feet tall. At this point I don't want to run out of fear that it will give chase, so I stay frozen. It looked at me and snarled, and I thought it was sizing me up and then all of a sudden it looks to the east, back at me one more time, and took two giant leaps toward the east, and onto the bank of the creek, that's about a 25 foot distance. It then jumps towards the treetops and disappears to the east.

Man meets Dogman in the woods, 2016

The walk went as planned, until I got about 300 yards south of the house. I stopped, to have a cigarette. My eyes started to wander, as I scoped for deer or coyote. As I gazed back and forth, I noticed this figure and froze. I literally froze! This thing made eye contact with me and then stood up. It was hairy, had very broad shoulders, and amber colored eyes. It let out a growl unlike any other I've heard. This wolf, as I call it, made two leaps and was gone.
The most surprising thing about this encounter was how silent the woods were, up to when I had my encounter.

Sparta Dogman sighting, 1987

It was dark, and they were on a rural road. Suddenly both of them saw something standing by the side of the road. In the headlights of the car, it appeared to be a human-like figure covered in grey fur. As they got closer and passed the figure, both of them got a very good look at it. It was the size of a man, stood on two legs, it was covered head to toe in grey fur, and had a wolf-like face. It even raised its hands and seemed to snarl at them as they drove by. They said it looked like a werewolf out of a Hollywood movie.

My two friends didn't dare stop, they continued driving. And of course they were peppering each other with questions, "Did you see that too?! Was that a dog? Was that someone dressed up in a costume?" and so on. As they are having this animated conversation, they pass by the sign that says "Welcome to Sparta" and drove through the small main street, and continued on out of the town in the direction of my cabin. Their conversation about what had just happened continued, when both of them looked up to see that same "Welcome to Sparta" sign AGAIN, followed by the same main street that they had just driven through only moments ago. They hadn't stopped or turned around. They had been traveling in the same direction on the same road, but somehow without any noticeable interruption in their journey, they had somehow been sent backwards several miles.

Huge dog-like creature grabbed deer, 1994

According to Ben, his third encounter with the creature took place in 1994 when he and a cousin were walking after dark in the direction of the beach from Lakeshore Drive along the edges of dunes. As the two watched a deer standing in a clearing, an enormous dog-like creature rapidly snatched the animal and carried it off into the brush.

"We went down to the spot, and you could see where the deer tracks ended," Ben said. "They vanished, leaving only tracks from that thing."

There is also a tale that in early 1994 a car on Lakeshore Drive was involved in a collision with a large animal. It is said the occupants of the vehicle were uninjured and police determined it was a deer strike. The tale includes a witness that claimed gray fur covered the grill of the wrecked vehicle, but no blood or animal carcass was found. It was said the driver couldn't explain what he hit.

Hofma Nature Preserve bipedal "dog", 1993

In 1993, after dark, Ben was hiking the trails in Hofma Nature Preserve with as many as four friends when, passing the float bridge near the center of the preserve, they heard a sound to their right. Ben spied what resembled a dog standing behind a tree on a ridge above, approximately 70 feet away.

"I thought it was just a dog walking along, then it stood up on its hind legs," Ben said. "One of its feet gripped a branch on the tree. Our eyes met and we just stared at each other for about five minutes, then it ran off."

Male werewolf on top of hill, 1973

Let me start with when I was a teenager- I was staying with my Uncle Jay and Aunt Shell in the summer of 1973. I was between my sophomore and junior year in high school. My Uncle drove a local grocery delivery truck, Pampania's I think, in the Flint Michigan area. I loved hanging out with him, driving around delivering produce, fruit, stuff like that. Every night we took the truck back to this fenced in truck park, and we drove home in his car. Well, late on a Thursday night (about 11:30), we were headed up the winding road that snaked around the hill up to the truck park, and we both saw what we thought was a big dog on the side of the road, pawing at something. As we got closer, I saw the thing was rooting and licking something with tongue and snout. Then the SOB stood up. This was no dog!

My Uncle slowed to a crawl (not quite stopping) and hit the high beams, and what I saw scared me so bad that I couldn't even get a scream out! It was a MAN, covered in short, black fur, clearly well muscled with the head of a German Shepherd or wolf. I could hardly breathe. It's eyes were yellowy-orange colored, a well muscled abdomen and thighs and was clearly (if you get my drift) a tugid MALE. We didn't make a sound but started to roll by, when it lunged across the access road in a single leap.

We got to the top of the hill, and my Uncle went into the guard hut in the middle of the fenced in area to turn in his keys and do whatever. He came back with the keys to the Ford and we drove back down the hill. As we neared the sight where we saw the dog-man, he pulled it over, and reached under the seat and got out a Colt Python .44 magnum handgun, checked the ammo in the revolver and told me to lock the door after him. I was not to do anything, including get out of the car, no matter what I was or heard, he said, and he was dead serious. After a few minutes, he called me to him, and he pointed to the side of the road.

There was a fresh (I know, I used to hunt and fish a lot) deer carcass, with the haunches torn away, and the poor things guts spilled out behind it. We just went home that night but were very careful the rest of the summer, never seeing the dog-man again.

Possible Dogman sighting, March 2015

A group of three people in Michigan reportedly came across an unidentified dog-like creature in the woods of St. Clair County.

The man reporting the sighting, a 46-year-old store manager who provided his full name but asked to remain anonymous, told Cryptozoology News that he and his son were walking through the woods with a friend when the creature showed up March 7.

According to the man, his son was the one able to catch a better glimpse of the alleged creature. He did not immediately reply to follow up questions regarding the age and name of the eyewitness. The report did not include the specific time of the event.

"Just as I got a glimpse the creature suddenly disappeared into the trees," his son said. "It had black fur. The tail was huge, it was at least 3 feet long."

The eyewitness says he is sure the being wasn't a dog because of the way it moved.

"It was not dog-like at all."

The purported creature, he said, was standing on four legs at the time of the sighting.

Oakland Co., Dogman next to road, 2017

"I was driving and looked at the side of the road because I saw something large move," the student reports about the mid-day encounter. "I noticed it right away."

The woman described the alleged humanoid as having a dog head and a man's body.

"It looked like a fit man, although covered slightly in hair. It had the head of a grey dog and was very tall," she added.

The creature, she explains, was "swaying back and forth".

"It was swaying strangely, like I have never seen a creature move before."

Hunched, mangy-looking creature,

A friend of mine were driving to 7/11 late at night, when a strange hunched back, large mangy creature ran across the road. The road is called Hospital Road in Waterford. The creature ran into the woods and we couldn't see it when we stopped. This was no normal dog. If it was a coyote then it's the biggest coyote I've ever seen…no this was much bigger, with a huge head and looked like it just crawled out of the deepest pits of hell.

Crouched quadrupedal Dogman, 2009

July 2009 I borrowed my father's Chevy Diesel truck to help my sister move. My father lives 10 miles SE of Fennville, MI. It was around 10:30 PM when I was on 118th street East of 58th when I saw a small herd of deer emerge on the right side of the road. I slowed way down when I saw them. Instead of crossing, they all perked their heads and stared across the road, but there was nothing there. At this point, I was about 200 yards away. I slowly approached the deer waiting for them to cross. I was about 50 feet away when "IT" came out from the tall weeds on the left hand side. It was on all fours but it looked like it was crouched on all fours. It was chocolate brown, had a bushy long tail (German Shepherd-like) Its fur was shaggy and unkempt and it had pointed ears, a wolf shaped head and it was baring its large pointed white teeth. My dad's truck is a large Duromax diesel pickup truck. This thing was crouched on all fours and its shoulder blades were still the same height as the driver side window. It was looking down at the ground (probably because of my hi-beams) as I passed by it. This is the only time in my life when I felt my life was in danger. I immediately hit the gas and took off.

Pack of 4-6 possible werewolves on four legs crossed highway, 1963

We were on the expressway...not sure which one and maybe in the Kalamazoo area. It was kind of a bleak day and I always was looking out of the window trying to spot deer. The highway was a little busy, but all of a sudden I saw a pack of animals...maybe 4 to 6 that went across the expressway, through both lines of traffic and went off into the woods...And, they went fast.

They were quite big, long and lanky and all of them were a gray color....in my mind they looked like a werewolf....that was like the shape they had. They went so fast...it seemed like I was the only one that saw them from our car. We talked about it a little bit and I just assumed they were timber wolves...even though I didn't know what timber wolves looked like at the time. Well, over the years I kind of forgot about it...but a couple of years ago I got on the internet and looked up Timberwolves. The animals I saw back in 1963 were not Timberwolves and it has stayed in my mind about who to tell what I saw.

Sighting between Kalamazoo and Battle Creek, 2006?

A person observed a nearly seven foot tall, upright canid standing near the road. When it turned and saw the car approaching, it quickly dropped to the ground and pulled itself into a 2-foot high cornfield, using its "long, lanky arms." Once safely in the field, it ran away on all fours "at lightning speed," leaving the witness shaken. Two other persons had observed the creature near there six months earlier.

Dogman/-men stalking youngsters, 2009

We were going a different way back, and this area is full of deer, cornfields, and dense woods.
It was a slow ride, and I heard something in a tree line next to the road to my left. (A cornfield was on the other side of the tree line)
I was looking into the dark, at what I thought was a deer. But It couldn't have been a deer; it was much larger, and seemed to come out of a tree.
It was snapping limbs like candles, the loud cracking and popping was enough to make most men pee themselves.
Most of my life, I have been interested in, and perused paranormal things, so my buddies were well aware that, when I say "run", or "get out of there", they take it seriously.
I yelled. I have never seen a fat kid (my best friend) ride a bike that fast in my life.
We managed to get away (to a well lit area with several houses) and were talking about what each of us had seen.
It was universal throughout the group, a large creature on two legs, that was on four. (Some of the group did not see it until it came out of the tree)
We did not know of the Michigan Dogman. We were quite unnerved, and I drew my knife. (I'm well known to carry my full size military Ka-Bar)
We walked, the bikes on our outsides, the people on the in, down the long road, surrounded in corn fields. (The crop circulation landed on corn this year)

We could hear multiple things just within the corn, and it was too dark to see.
We got about a mile a way, and were turning a bend. There was an opening (for tractors) to my right, that opened up to a corn field.
Three things stared at us.
Three things tall enough to be out of the corn.
Dark, reflective eyes stared back at us. I did not alert my friends to this. I simply watched them, and kept it to myself.

Washtenaw Co. Several Sightings, 2005/2015/2017

I walked towards the sound and remember hearing the creature flinch because the movement stopped as I approached. I called out for the golden retriever and peered into the trees. The barn had spotlights facing the house and with the white paint job on it, they created a glow that allowed me to see better. About 7 feet off the ground, a long muzzle poked through the trees. Followed by the full-figure of this creature. It was only 20 feet away from me, so I got the full picture. It was tall and lean but very muscular. It had a distinct brown pelt on its body, with blackish fur on its shoulders. It had huge paws for feet, but its hands looked like they had 5 fingers, so they resembled long human hands, except for the fur and claws on them. Its head was the scariest. This thing had a huge set of canines. It looked like it was snarling, but I believe it was trying to smile. I couldn't make out exactly what its eye color was because of how dark it was, but they pierced into my soul! As the creature came into full view, I remember saying out loud to myself, "Werewolf!" I backed up slowly and the creature stood there, like a proud man standing over a deer he had hunted. It watched me for about 30 seconds, but it felt like 30 minutes. That's when my father, uncle, cousin, and grandfather all came out of the barn. When I tell you this thing ran, I mean it RAN! It turned around, dropped to all 4's, and leaped into the forest, making only a slight noise.

Dogman sighting, 2008

Two glowing yellow eyes. I stopped with the lights on it. The figure was hard to make out. It was the eyes that freaked me out. They were low, then they went high…very high. Then back down like the creature was crouching then standing up. It didn't run it just kept moving up and down. I watched for about 10 minutes and got scared.

I pulled into the garage. Door down and all locked. Put my beautiful secluded home up for sale that summer and moved. The location was surrounded by woods fields and swamps. The creature I saw was very big, black with a wolf head. But bigger than a wolf. It was a werewolf. The body resembled a hyena. I know Dogman is real.

Cass Co. Rural Dogman, 2001

It was the fall of 2001, late fall. All the leaves were gone. My stepdaughter and I were looking out the french doors to see a creature....black in color, like a big bear with haunches and the head of a wolf. It was walking up the hill behind my house. It was on all fours and walked like a panther...stalking. I had never seen anything like it in my life. The only word that describes it is werewolf. Now at night periodically....I can hear something in the 20 acre plus swamp in the middle of the night. Very loud and splashing around. It has the scream of an infant...Loud and hysterical. I live in a very rural and secluded area in Southwest Michigan...Cass County.

Roscommon, Michigan

It was me and my buddy and we were in Roscommon, Michigan. We were on our way out into the woods for our evening hunt. The hunt went well. We saw the normal 2 or 3 deer but we couldn't get a shot. So we left a little early because we were irritated. We put our stuff in the back of the truck. My buddy heard some rustling in the woods behind us. So me and my buddy got our flashlights out of the truck and when we shined our light into the brush, we saw two huge red glowing eyes about 7 feet up off the ground. We followed them down and all we could see was a massive dog's foot sticking out of the brush so we ran to the truck in fear. When the lights turned on we saw a dog that stood upright about 7 feet tall and we started driving away and we never saw it again and it had to be the scariest experience of our lives.

Near Sault Ste. Marie, 2011

A few years ago, around midnight, I was on my way home to Sault Ste. Marie, MI. On I-75, a couple hundred yards south of the Bay Road overpass in Mackinac County, I noticed something move near the highway reflectors. Thinking it was a deer I turned on the bright lights and watched for it to cross the road. As I approached it I notice that what I thought was the reflectors on the highway was orange, and then it blinked on and off like an eye. Thinking, "what the heck is that?" I sped up to get closer. As I got closer I could see the silhouette of the animal. It was sitting like a dog, its head was even with the reflectors. It stood on all 4s and turned and walked down in the ditch then up a little incline then turned and looked at my truck. It turned back to the highway walked on all 4s to the shoulder of the blacktop looked at the truck again with those orange eyes. The eyes were huge. It then jumped to within a foot or two of the center line, and then the next jump landed in the grass on the shoulder of the road. I was probably like 100 feet from it. This animal was rippling in muscles, and looked like it weighed around 500 pounds if not more. Its hair which covered its body looked short and its head was huge with hardly no neck. After I passed were it crossed I hit the brakes, as there were no cars on the highway, and started to back up. As I got close to the spot where it crossed I suddenly felt fear and thought, "What the hell am I doing?" I put the truck back in drive and began to leave. As I was rolling the window up I glanced back and noticed a light, bright like a flood light, ascending into the sky at a high rate of speed. It was at a angle of about 1 o'clock and in just a few seconds was out of sight. Something else that was strange was there were not any light rays trailing it.

Houghton Lake, 2010

Ok well in Houghton Lake, Michigan in 2010 I went camping with my dad and my brother. We went out to the real woods not just a campsite. It was somewhere around noon and we started to hear coyotes yelp and howl. My dad said that coyotes are never out this early. My dad howled at them and they howled back. My dad thought maybe they were sick and looking for food. He said that they'd do anything for food if they were sick. I didn't know about the legend of the Dogman during that time. But now I'm starting to wonder if maybe it was the Dogman. It came to be bedtime for me and my brother but my dad stayed up by the fire. He woke us up early at like 3 or 4 am and made us go in the truck and sleep there for the rest of the night because the sounds were only like twenty feet away. I asked him the next day to howl at them and he said no because he didn't want them to come eat us. He said that next time he is gonna bring a gun just in case.

Near Luther, 2010

My dad and I were out hunting near Luther and we were on this hill in the woods. There was this tree that was fork-shaped. I saw something standing there but dad didn't. It looked like a wolf that was standing up. I couldn't see him well because it was about 30 yards away and there was foliage around it. I didn't tell my dad because he would have told me I was seeing things.

I shot at it with my bb gun to see what it would do. It just moved a little and still stared at us. I can't believe my dad didn't see it, but he did not have his glasses that day. We walked away and I turned around and I didn't see him. I know what he looked like because I saw the artist's rendition of him. He had the same ears as the picture. I had the crap scared out of me!

Walking in the Woods, 2009

I was walking the woods with my boyfriend one day and I saw something run in front of me at a distance. It did startle me but at first I thought it was nothing so we just kept walking. I saw it again and it startled me even more because I didn't know what it was at the time. It looked like a dog and a man at the same time. It didn't dawn on me at the time but after a few minutes of thinking of it I remembered the legend of the Michigan Dogman. My boyfriend just laughed at me when I told him I wanted to go home because he didn't believe me.
  We started to walk further away in the woods when my boyfriend saw it. He decided to turn around and go home. The closer we got to my house it seemed that the figure got closer and closer. I looked behind us 3 or 4 times but the very last time I looked at the figure it started to run after us so we ran all the way home... We never went into those woods ever again!

Cadillac, 2009

I recently recalled an experience from my childhood that had been repressed in my mind since I was about 4 or 5 years old. As a child, I grew up on a 20 acre lot just on the outskirts of Cadillac. At that time there was more tree coverage and fewer industrial sites in the area; we were mostly surrounded by woods.

One early summer morning I had gotten up before dawn to watch my Dad get ready to go off to work. Some mornings he'd get up at 3:30 to 4:00 a.m. to start his days. Me and my Mom would get up and send him on his way; daily routine back then. He'd always put on his work pants and work shirts over his regular clothes and proceed to go out to his truck and load his equipment for the day. His work clothes were the dark and mossy looking material; really coarse feeling. In the darkness he'd look really shaggy looking.

The morning of my encounter I had gotten up a little earlier than usual and was very groggy. I stumbled to the large plate glass window and saw something rummaging in the truck's bed over the side of the truck. I assumed it was just dad so I banged on the window to get his attention and wave. I was chilled to the bone by what peered back at me. A creature that stood on two feet but for the life of me had the head of a dog; canine-like but yet somehow human. We locked eyes for what seemed to be an eternity. Strangely enough though the eyes were not yellow as everyone else seems to see. They were a pale yellow/green in color.

I finally mustered a scream and fell backwards off the couch in front of the window. As I was falling backwards the creature had already hit all fours and was lunging for the window. He started at a good twenty feet away at the trucks back end. My scream had gotten my dad out of the bathroom and into the living room yelling to my mom to hush me up. He looked out the window and asked me what I saw but I was just sobbing. He went to the front door and turned on the porch light and found nothing. Annoyed that his morning was off to a not-so-quiet start, he made my mother take me back to bed and he left for the day.

I was so traumatized by this experience I repressed it for all these years. It took looking up the Dogman and studying cryptozoolgy to kick the memory loose again. The house where this took place still stands but the tree coverage that was abundant as a child is history. Whatever that thing is, I'm sure he's still out there waiting.

Hunting, 2009

It was November 15th and me and my dad were heading to our deer blinds. It was around 6:30, it was very dark and foggy and you could only see a few feet in front of you. I got in my blind and got ready, then about 10 minutes later I heard something running behind me. I got scared because deer shouldn't be awake. Then I could see something down the road, it looked like a bear but it was standing up on two feet. Then it stopped and it looked like it sniffed the air, I hoped it didn't smell me because it was looking right at me. Then it just ran off the other way, I finally got the nerve to call my dad to come get me. Then I told him what happened. He told me that he saw 2 coyotes and that my cousin shot one. Something was weird - we never see coyotes out where we were hunting, but all of a sudden there were 3. It was like there was a coyote frenzy going on.

Topinabee, 2009

A few years back in Topinabee, Michigan my uncle was coming home from work he had just passed the Indian river golf course leading into Topinabee and suddenly this huge black object ran across the road.

Traverse City, 2009

Me and my friend Aris were in the woods by Traverse City Christian School and then out of the corner of our eyes we saw something like bigfoot. We thought it was the DOGMAN, so we ran back to our cross country group

Dogman Hits Car

In early 1994, a car on Lakeshore Drive was involved in a collision with a large animal. The occupants of the vehicle were uninjured, and police were reported to have determined it was a deer strike. Witnesses said there was gray fur all over the front of the wrecked vehicle, but no blood, or animal carcass was found. One witness was reported to say, "The driver couldn't even explain what he hit."

Rockford, Two Sightings

e:1= I was taking my dogs to go to the bathroom at 3:00am and i decided to go out there with them so they don't run away. I was out in my front yard when i heard a growl from the side of my house. I quickly looked over and there was a rustle in the bushes, I saw a tail and a leg and it was gone. I was really f****** scared. (i am 13 btw) I took my dogs in and went to bed although i didn't get much sleep that night.

e:2= In my backyard if you go strait you go over to a hill and to my friends house, if you go left you go into the forest. I was over at my friends house and I didn't realize what the time was. It was 11:38 and I said i had to go home. As I left me and him were joking about wolves eating me (because both of our houses are covered by forest) and we laughed for a few seconds and i headed over the hill. As i got to the top there was a deep growl from the forest and I looked over and saw the eyes. It was too dark to see the Dogmans body so I ran off really f****** scared. He was chasing me and I could hear him behind me. I got to my front door and glanced behind me and the Dogman was gone. I heard a long howl (I know the dogman doesn't really howl so it may of just been a wolf) and i went inside with a hell of a lot of memories inside of my head that shouldn't of been.
I still have nightmares about it to this day.

A Drive, 2008

The way that this story all fell together for me is just way too weird for this story to be untrue.

About three years ago, my cousin, Mike, and I were dropping off his girlfriend and her friend after seeing a movie. It was about 11 o'clock and we were going down this long gravel road that stemmed off another back-county road. The long gravel road was about two miles long and it led directly to his girlfriend's house (it was basically her driveway).

After dropping them off and heading back up the driveway we saw something off the side of the road about a hundred yards or so away. At first we just figured it was some sort of animal, so we flashed the brights on and off to scare it away.

Once we got closer, maybe 20 yards away, we realized this wasn't anything we had ever seen before. Whatever it was stood up. Its back was massive and hunched over and its legs were very skinny. When it looked at us, its eyes glowed in the headlights. Scared to death, I just looked down. I did not want to look at this thing, I was way to terrified. My cousin and I both sat there panicking.

"Do we turn the headlights off?"
"What if we lose sight of it?"

"Do we just turn the car off and let this thing walk away?"
"What if there's another one and we can't start the car and get away fast enough?"

"Do we hit it and keep driving?"
"What if we don't kill it and it sits on the hood and tries to get into the car?"

As we both sat there in terror, I continued to watch it out the top of my eyes. There was no way that I was going to look directly at this, or if there's another one, I don't want to see it either. All I could really see of it was its skinny dog-like legs and its massive upper body. It stood there for a second and then just walked into the woods... ON TWO LEGS!!

Up until a while ago, when I told people about it, I told them that the only thing I remember were the way its eyes shined back, its large, hunched over back, and its skinny "dog-like" legs. When my cousin and I talked about it, we just tried to conclude that maybe it was a deformed bear or something. We had never heard of the Michigan Dogman before.

The part where this story gets weird is when I was talking to my friends back at home, just a few weeks ago, we were trying to get together a ghost hunting trip for when I came home on leave from San Diego with the Marines. I was online searching for Michigan hauntings, and Michigan paranormal activity, and I came across this story titled, "Michigan Dogman." The police reports, the witness accounts, the drawings, everything matched perfectly. It was crazy to me that other people had seen what I saw that night. It had been about three years since then and it was insane that just now I'm finding such a perfect explanation.

A Farm Outside of Corunna, 2008

I don't know if this will be helpful but it's interesting.
I live in Sarnia, Ontario, on the Canadian side of the Michigan border. Almost 2 months ago a police officer friend of my husbands told him about being called out to a farm outside of Corunna, still on the border but further down river, to examine some horses. What he found was 6 horses in a corral that had bled to death from huge claw marks to their neck and shoulder areas. There had been reports of a lynx on the native reserve outside of town and a young boar black bear had been trapped and moved from about 100 km. away from this incident but these predators don't kill like that, they will kill 1 prey, drag it away and cache it, then go back for another; these horses died where they were attacked. Just another one of those strange stories with no immediate explanation, I suppose.

Outside of Bedroom, 2008

Incident occurred late July, 2008 approximately 1.30 a.m. The neighbor's dog started barking and running back and forth along the side of our houses. After 15 minutes I became weary from the noise and got out of bed to take a look at what was causing the commotion. It was a clear, warm night without cloud cover, and I don't remember seeing the Moon. I slid open the sliding door from our bedroom to the backyard and patio/pool area. I turned left towards my neighbors' house which is about 15-20 feet from my bedroom. There is a concrete enclosure next to our bedroom that houses the air conditioner and pool machinery. As I stepped out of the bedroom and took a couple of steps, I was greeted by guttural growl coming from the other side of the enclosure that I could not see. It was frightening and froze me in my tracks. I was scared. I have never heard anything like it except in the Hollywood Werewolf movies. It was definitely saying don't make another move or else, you get ripped apart, you will die. At least that's what I felt. I was born and raised in Detroit and lived on the near-westside on 12th Street and Burlingame. We had rough tough guys in those days and a white boy living in a black neighborhood is something like daily combat. I didn't scare easily but I was terrified this night.

I didn't see anything the next morning such as tracks on the pavement. It was not feline nor was it a bear, both of which can be found where we live. Also, it was not a coyote which I have seen many in the early a.m. out hunting as close as ten feet away carrying small prey in their mouths. I used to take my wife for medical treatment three times a week at 3.00 a.m. for eight years so I had many encounters with these animals and I repeat a coyote it was not. I know, I could have taken ten or 15 steps and found out what the mystery was, however mama didn't raise no fool and I didn't have a Colt 45 with six silver in the chamber and six silver in a speed-loader so I let it slide. There was one reported incident in the 1980's in Valencia which is next to Castaic where my family was living. A couple of teenage boys were camping out one night and were harried by what they reported to the police as a dogman-like creature that stood upright and ran on two feet and was covered with dark shaggy hair.

That's my story, it is nothing but the truth. I was born in Detroit and lived there until 1966 when I moved to California and I never heard anything about the dogman. My cousin attended Ferris State in Big Rapids and he never mentioned the dogman legend to me. In addition I went to summer camp in Port Huron one year when I was in high school, Camp Ozenham or something like that spelling and this was the perfect place for a dogman to live but nothing was ever mentioned about. Michigan is a perfect place for a dogman creature to live, plenty of green and fresh water with a moderate population as opposed to CA where fresh water would definitely be a major problem for survival.

Luther, 1997

I don't know if this really counts as we didn't see anything but it was close enough. My grandparents own a farm in Luther, MI with a large patch of pines behind their home. One evening, maybe 1997, my dad and I went for a walk in those woods. My dad wanted to, I didn't so much due to hour and the woods already being dark. As we entered the woods my dad tried to scare me by making a howling noise (coincidentally enough we had just heard the Legend song a few days prior). I hit him and told him that wasn't funny. He chuckled saying there is no such thing, it's just a story. I grumbled saying even stories have some bit of truth in them. We walked on into the woods, eventually losing the little bit of daylight that remained outside the woods. Then we heard a screaming howl come from the back of my grandpa's property, maybe a quarter mile away. I again told my dad that wasn't funny and he said it wasn't him. It happened again. Only this time, it was closer. Whatever made the sound, and it was the same sound just louder, was moving, fast, too. We didn't hear anything that sounded like movement in the tree or underbrush but I was certain something was out there. We continued our merry little walk through the woods, much to my chagrin, but we didn't hear another thing from the woods, though the entire time I felt like I was being watched by something that didn't like me or want me there.

The thing that sets it off is this woods are very close to the cabin that was scratched up in Luther, MI, so this is obviously its area to be in. I think this occurred in '97 due the frequency of the song being played on the radio, so this may the 7th year prophecy fulfilled.
Well this is my encounter, hope it's to your liking, as much as it freaks me out.

Sledding, 2008

I was out sledding on a snowbank my dad had made plowing. I was out there for maybe 35 min. and I went down the hill and went further due to a packed path. I went and as I got up out of my sled, I saw a footprint. It was 10-12 inches and had claws also. I went inside and told my mom she didn't believe me.

PHOTOS OF DOGMEN

Photos of Dogmen from Around the World

Nearly everyone these days has a camera on them, and even our cell phones have cameras on them. With these high-tech compact devices we are able to take them out and take a quick snapshot or short video of something we are interested in. Imagine walking through the woods or driving your car and running across a dogman. You first instinct would be fight or flight but the following photos were taken from those who were brave enough to pause and capture the primal fear moment of their encounters.

Type 3 Variant-1

Type 3 Variant-3

Type 3 Variant-4

Type 3 Variant-4

Canine Variant-1

Canine Variant-2 (Hyena) smiling up at photographer.

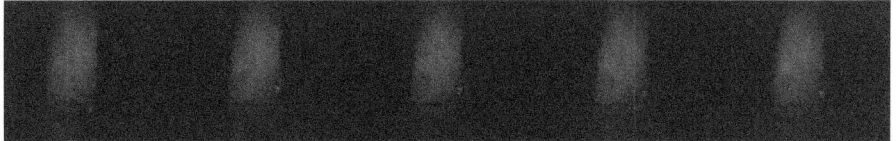

Canine Variant-2 (Hyena) Spotted hiding behind tree. Was watching two boys while they hunted for frogs. White teeth smile can be seen.

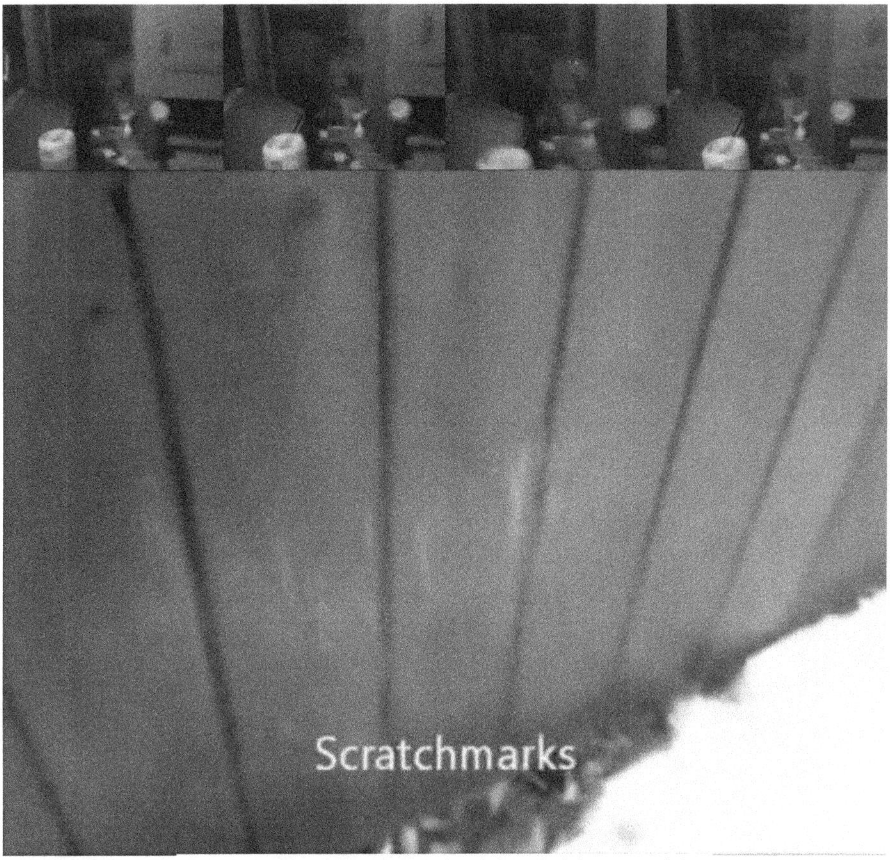

Canine Variant-3 peaks in Michigan cabin.

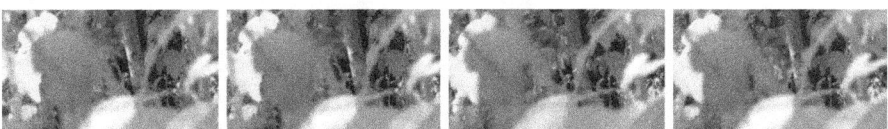

Canine Variant-3 Watches cameraman from bushes.

Canine Variant-3 in Northern California

Canine Variant-3 staring at cameraman

Canine Variant-3 in Brazil

Canine Variant-3 followed person home and starred in bedroom window at him.

Canine Variant-3 photographed by security guard in Michigan.

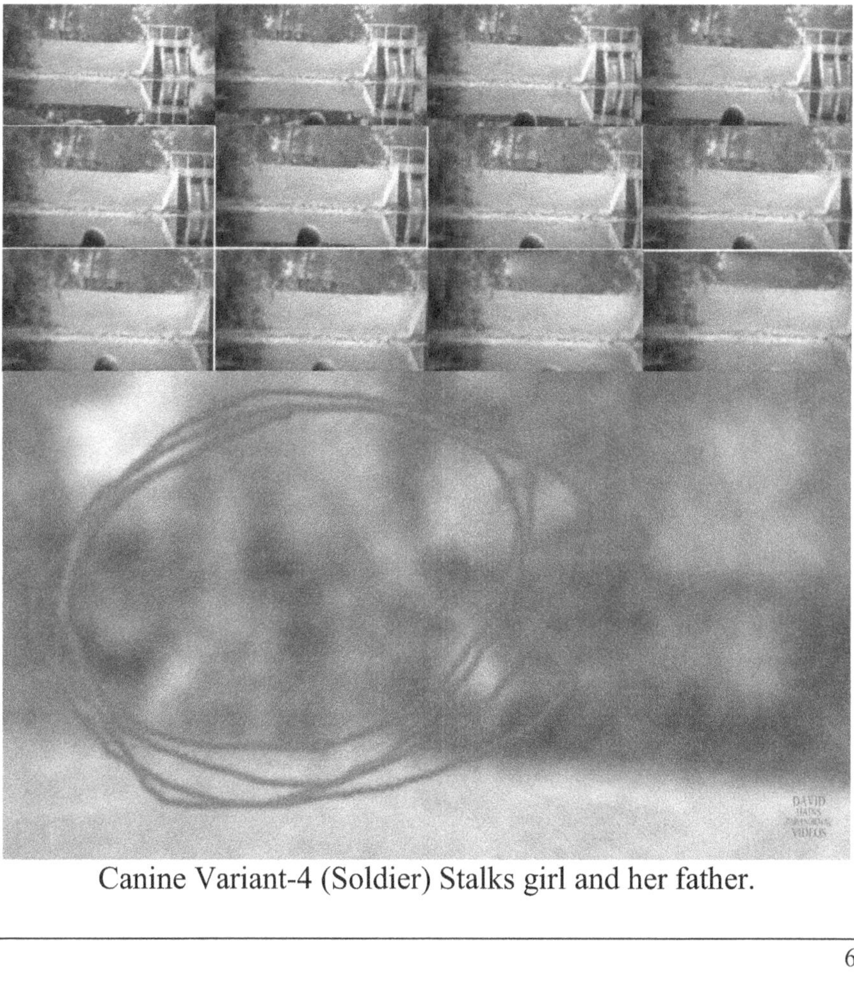

Canine Variant-4 (Soldier) Stalks girl and her father.

Canine Variant-4 (Soldier)

Newspaper Clippings from the United States

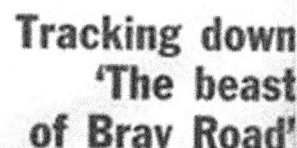

63

The Seattle Daily Times
12th EXTRA

MYSTERIOUS BEAST
Stalked In Wallingford

[article text illegible]

Forest City

Sunday, August 02, 2009

Campers Missing, Terror At

Saturday night the local Sheriff's Department and the US Fish And Game Officers were called to the Puzzle Creek Swamp Campground to investigate a disturbance in the Campground.

When the officers arrived they discovered a camp site where two teenage boys had been spending the night had been torn apart and large amounts of blood were observed on the ground and on the trees overhead. Some blood was on trees as high as 12 foot high.

Other people in the campground reported that a large creature that looked like a Big Foot or Sasquatch came out of the woods around 10 pm and attacked the two teen age boys staying at the camp site.

People staying in the campground said the creature threw a teenage boy over each shoulder and then ran off back into the swamp. As of press time today a massive search is under way for the teenage boys bodies. The State Medical Examiner stated that with the amount of blood found he does not think either boy could have survived the attack. The teenage boys names are being with

Beware the 'Beast of Truro'
Mysterious Creature Has Mauled Animals in Cape Cod

TRURO, Mass. — Who or what is the "Beast of Truro?" Is it a mountain lion preying on local pets and livestock, a dog or pack of dogs, an ocelot, a lynx, a wildcat or some yet unidentified creature?

The purported beast, Cape Cod's answer to Big Foot and the Loch Ness Monster, has been a major topic of conversation and news articles since last fall.

The first evidence that some unknown predator was loose came when a dozen dead cats were found in the same area in Truro in September. Two weeks ago, a 175-pound hog was so badly mauled, its flanks ripped by deep claw marks and a chunk of flesh ripped out of its neck, that it had to be killed. A few days later, two pigs were clawed in their pens.

The most dramatic description came from William and Marsha Medeiros of Truro. They said they were taking a walk about three months ago on the bike trail near Head of the Meadow Beach in Truro when the animal appeared 50 feet in front of them.

Mrs. Medeiros continued:

"My husband put his arm out to stop me and said, 'You see what I see?' Together we said, 'It's not a fox.' It had a very definite long ropelike tail like the letter J. It hit the ground and went up. We figured it was about as tall as up to our knees and weighed 60 or 80 pounds."

Medeiros left the path to get a branch to protect them. The creature did not rush for cover, Mrs. Medeiros said, but walked slowly and casually luctant to report what they had seen. "Who would believe it?" Mrs. Medeiros said.

Others have reported hearing strange catlike cries in the night. Edward Oswalt, a Truro Selectman and health officer, said a New York man called in mid-December to say he had seen "something resembling a mountain lion" in North Truro.

Oswalt and seashore officers have made efforts to identify the culprit by its tracks near the pigpens, but in the sandy soil they could find no clear impressions. Oswalt said the "general consensus is that the beast is a dog or dogs, but I don't know if you can put that together with what happened." Could it be a mountain lion? "That seems far out, but it's not impossible," he replied.

Werewolf Case In Defiance Not Viewed Lightly By Police

Chief Cites Concern Over Reported Sightings Of Large Beast, Attack

By JAMES STEGALL
Blade Staff Writer

DEFIANCE, O. — Some people here are jokingly referring to it as the case of the werewolf. But Defiance police are serious about it.

Three persons have told police that they saw a large, beast that resembles a werewolf lurking along railroad tracks near downtown Defiance in the last week.

In each case he was spotted during the early morning hours, and one man, a train crewman switching trains, said that he was approached from behind and was struck on the shoulder with a piece of 2-by-4 lumber. But when he ran the "werewolf" also disappeared into some nearby brush.

In the other reported incidents the "werewolf" was seen by another train crewman about 3 a.m. Police say the third report came from a motorist who said "it" ran in front of his car about 4 a.m. and then quickly disappeared.

"We don't know what to think," Police Chief Donald Breckler said. "We didn't release it (to the news media) when we got the first report about a week ago. But now we're taking it seriously. We're concerned for the safety of our people."

Chief Breckler said that descriptions of the "werewolf" given by the three persons (police are not giving their names) that spotted him are similar. But he admits in each case the description is "vague."

"Very hairy" is the first description given by each person who saw the "werewolf." The chief said that he thinks that a person is wearing some disguise such as a mask. "But there is a lot of natural hair, too," he said.

"I'm inclined to think it might be a local person," Chief Breckler said. "None of the other area towns have had anything like this. And in each case he has been seen in the same area of our town."

Chief Breckler said that the creature wears dark clothing and at first reports described him as ranging from 7 to 9 feet tall. "But that was a little exaggerated," the chief said.

Two of the trainmen that reported seeing the "werewolf" work in the area during the early morning hours. Both of them are from Toledo. The third complaint came from a local grocery store employee, Mr. Breckler said.

"If his motive is robbery then he is not picking on the type of person that would have a lot of money," Chief Breckler said. "We don't know what his motive is."

INDEX

	Page
Business News	55
Obituaries	36
Sports	50
Stocks	51
Weather and Log	18
Women's News	12

Lyrics to 'The Legend'

A drawing by Steve Cook, WTCM radio announcer and production director, shows what the fictitious half man, half dog might look like. Cook said the song is a concoction of numerous stories he's heard over the years.

A cool summer mornin' in early June is when the legend began,
At a nameless logging camp in Wexford County where the Manistee River ran.
Eleven lumberjacks near the Garland Swamp found an animal they thought was a dog.
In a playful mood they chased it around 'til it ran inside a hollow log.
A logger named Johnson grabbed him a stick and poked around inside.
Then the thing let out an unearthly scream and came out and stood upright.
None of those men ever spoke very much about whatever happened then.
They just packed up their belongings and left that night and were never heard from again.
It was 10 years later in '97 when a farmer near Buckley was found
Slumped over his plow, his heart had stopped.
There were dog tracks all around.
Seven years past the turn of the century they say a crazy old widow had a dream
Of dogs that circled her house at night.
They walked like men and screamed.
In 1917 a sheriff who was out a walkin' found a driverless wagon and tracks in the dust like wolves had been a stalkin'.
Near the roadside a four-horse team lay dead with their eyes open wide.
When the vet finished up his examination he said it looked like they died from fright.
In '37 a schooner captain said several crew members had reported
A pack of wild dogs roaming Bowers Harbor.
His story was never recorded.
A man of the cloth in '57 found claw marks on an old church door.
The newspaper said they were made by a dog.
He'd a had to stood 7 foot 4.
In '67 a van load of hippies told a park ranger named Quinlin they'd been awakened in the night by a scratch at the winda . . . there was a dog man lookin' in and grinin'.
In '77 there were screams in the night near the village of Bellaire
Could have been a bobcat, could have been the wind. Nobody looked up there.
So far this spring no stories have appeared.
Have the dogmen gone away? Have they disappeared?
Soon enough I guess we'll know 'cause summer is almost here.
And in this decade called the '80s . . . the 7th year is here.
And somewhere in the northwoods darkness a creature walks upright
And the best advice you may ever get . . . is don't go out at night.

ARKANSAS GAZETTE, Tues., Nov. 27, 1973. ● 5A

Nonbeliever at Fouke Spots 'Monster' in Cow Pasture

FOUKE (AP) — Orville Scoggins, a farmer who has scoffed at tales of a Fouke monster, said he, his son, and grandson saw the creature in his field Sunday morning.

He said the "monster" was about four feet tall, stood upright and had "long pitch black hair."

There were so many reports last year of a strange creature in the area that a legend about the "Fouke monster" was born. A Texarkana film maker made a successful movie, "The Legend of Boggy Creek" about the sightings.

Scoggins, 67, told Fouke Constable Ernest Walraven that the three were helping one of his cows deliver a calf about 7:30 a.m. when he heard several cows bellowing.

"I looked up to see what the noise was and there it was about 100 yards away walking to the east," he said.

The field where the creature allegedly was sighted is about four miles east of Fouke and about a half mile south of the Rocky Mound Church, Walraven said.

Several tracks were found near the spot where Scoggins said he saw the creature. The tracks reportedly had a span of about 5½ inches in diameter and were 40 inches apart.

The owner and manager of Boggy Creek cafe at Fouke, Billy Williams, who is a friend of Scoggins, said, "Orvile was always one of our worst believers. He always made fun of the Fouke monster."

Youth Grilled as 'Werewolf' Suspect

The modern counterpart of a medieval torture chamber, in which a slim, attractive, young girl writhed for hours before her brutal murder by a maniacal "werewolf" killer, was sought by homicide detectives today.

The butchered torso, hacked in two at the waist, was found yesterday in a vacant lot on a Los Angeles "lover's lane."

Like the victims of predatory killers assuming the form of a wolf in ancient folklore, the body was gashed and mutilated almost beyond recognition.

HAGERSTOWN, MD., FRIDAY, MAY 5, 1871.

THE TENNESSEE WILDMAN

The Jackson (Tenn.) *Whig* of the 13th instant says: "We learn that between Sobby and Crainsville, on what is called Piney, in McNairy county, a strange and frightful being has been observed for several weeks. He is said to be seven feet high, and possessed of great muscular power. His eyes are unusually large, and fiery red; his hair hangs in a tangled and matted mass of jet below his waist, and his beard reaches below his middle. His entire body is covered with hair, and his whole aspect is most frightful. He shuns the sight of men, but approaches with wild and horrid screams of delight every woman who is unaccompanied by a man. He sometimes, with great caution, approaches houses, and should he see a man he runs away with astonishing swiftness, leaping the tallest fences with the ease of a deer, defying alike the pursuit of men and dogs. He has frightened several women by attempting to carry them off, as well as by his horrid aspect, and the whole country around Sobby is in consternation. The citizens are now scouring the woods, and are determined either to capture of drive off the monster.

Monroe's Monster

The recent doings at Monroe, Mich., may be taken as gratifying evidence that America is not going to wholly neglect the monster business. We on this side of the water have never had anything comparable to Scotland's famed Loch Ness monster, or even Tibet's Abominable Snowman. The Monster of Monroe is a start.

A couple of young ladies in the area claim to have had frightening but not tragic (an important point!) encounters with a large, hairy creature. In response, thousands of the curious have come to do a bit of monster-hunting. Restaurants, service stations and the like have been doing Saturday night business in midweek.

If the local people work it right, the way the canny folk around Loch Ness do, this can become a perennial shot in the arm for business. We anticipate more tidings about the Monster of Monroe.

References

The Werewolf Page Myths - Michigan DogMan, werewolfpage.com/myths/michigan_dogman.htm.

Weird Michigan - Ridgeway Monster, Michigan Dog Man, Shapeshifters, Dog Soldiers, www.weirdmichigan.com/monsters.html.

Sightings Log, Werewolf, Manwolf, Beast of Bray Road Home Page; Manwolf, Werewolf, Manimal, Dog Man, Manbeast, Bearwolf, Lizard Man, Smaller Bigfoot, www.beastofbrayroad.com/sightingslog2.html.

"Author: Legend of the Dog Man Still Haunts the Woods of Michigan." *Year of Michigan's Dogman: Stories & Encounters*, www.griswoldmountain.com/dogman_stories.htm.

Bachman, Michael. "'Dogman' Sighting in Michigan?" *Cryptozoology News*, 10 Apr. 2015, cryptozoologynews.com/dogman-sighting-in-michigan/.

Bachman, Michael. "Michigan Woman Claims Dogman Sighting." *Cryptozoology News*, 17 July 2017, cryptozoologynews.com/michigan-woman-claims-dogman-sighting/.

"Cryptic Fever." *Michigan Dogman Sighting - Reed City, MI / 1993*, crypticfever.yolasite.com/encounters-and-sightings/michigan-dogman-sighting-reed-city-mi-1993. "Dogman Encounters (Report Your Dogman Encounters Here!)." *Dogman Encounters*, www.dogmanencounters.com/#!manisteecounty-michigan/d28n4.

"Dogman Encounters (Report Your Dogman Encounters Here!)." *Dogman Encounters*, www.dogmanencounters.com/#!oceanacounty-michigan/onghk.

Ghtribune. "Legendary Dogman Seen in Ottawa County?" *Grand Haven Tribune*, 16 Sept. 2013, www.grandhaventribune.com/News/2013/09/16/Legendary-Dogman-seen-in-Ottawa-County.html.

Godfrey, Linda. "Cass County Croucher Creature." *Lindagodfrey's Blog*, 31 Mar. 2018, lindagodfrey.com/2018/03/18/cass-county-croucher-creature/.

Manning, Kieran. "The Clearest Dogman Images Ever Captured." The Clearest Dogman Images Ever Captured, YouTube, 25 Dec. 2017, www.youtube.com/watch?v=N0lsphVB7u0.

"New Pictures of the Michigan Dogman? (And Another Look at the Gable Film) , Page 3." *AboveTopSecret.com*, www.abovetopsecret.com/forum/thread349828/pg3#pid7375513.

"Oceana County, MI Encounter." *Dogman Encounters*, dogmanencounters.com/oceana-county-mi-encounter-2/.

"UnresolvedMysteries - The Michigan Dogman." *Reddit*, www.reddit.com/r/UnresolvedMysteries/comments/3pjrtz/the_michigan_dogman/cw89c2a/.

"Saginaw County, MI Encounter." *Dogman Encounters*, dogmanencounters.com/saginaw-county-mi-encounter/.

"The Legend of Michigans Dogman." *Creepypasta Wiki*, creepypasta.fandom.com/wiki/The_Legend_of_Michigans_Dogman.

Unknown. "Michigan Sightings." *DFRO (Dogman Field Research Organization)*, www.dogmanresearch.com/2013/04/michigan-sightings.html.

"Washtenaw County, MI Encounter." *Dogman Encounters*, dogmanencounters.com/washtenaw-county-mi-encounter/.

"Werewolves in the Trees?" *Lindagodfrey's Blog*, 10 Feb. 2017, lindagodfrey.com/2017/02/10/werewolves-in-the-trees/.

CPSIA information can be obtained
at www.ICGtesting.com
Printed in the USA
LVHW110612080223
738889LV00004B/678